Threads of Bliss

Weaving tales with a sock and shoe,
A snail in a top hat, how do you do?
Kites in the air, made of jelly beans,
Dance with the breeze, like wobbly machines.

A spoon sings loud, while the forks tap dance,
Chasing the shadows, giving friends a chance.
An octopus rides a bicycle, oh dear!
In this wild quilt, there's nothing to fear.

Dancing on Cloud Nine

Footloose mice in tiny blue shoes,
Twirl on the clouds, singing the blues.
While rainbows spin from marshmallow fluff,
With giggles and wiggles, it's more than enough.

A frog with a crown leads the parade,
While grasshoppers hop, unafraid.
Their polka-dot suits, a dazzling sight,
In this wacky dance, everything feels right.

Original title:
A Perfectly Happy Ending

Copyright © 2024 Creative Arts Management OÜ
All rights reserved.

Author: Ryan Rogers
ISBN HARDBACK: 978-9916-94-900-9
ISBN PAPERBACK: 978-9916-94-901-6

Sunsets in Bloom

The sun dips low, a golden show,
With squirrels dancing, don't you know?
A cat in shades, on a skateboard rides,
While laughter echoes, and joy abides.

Pineapple pizza, a feast quite rare,
Unicorns prance with a breeze in their hair.
The flowers giggle, the sky does beam,
It's a wacky world, like a silly dream.

Tides of Contentment

Seashells chuckle, as waves come to play,
Fish wear bow ties, it's a stylish day.
Jellyfish waltz on the ocean floor,
While starfish gossip, who could ask for more?

A treasure chest holds giggles and grins,
As sandcastles brag about their wins.
Coconuts giggle, sharing the sand,
In this quirky realm, all feels so grand.

The Calm after the Storm

Raindrops danced on muddy streets,
While squirrels wore tiny, soggy cleats.
Sun peeks out, a wink so sly,
Puddles mirror a bright blue sky.

Umbrellas flipped, a carnival show,
As folks slip-slide, forth they go.
Laughter bursts, a joyful cheer,
Storm clouds fade, it's clear, oh dear!

Kites now soar, birds take flight,
Dancing in the warmth of light.

A Symphony of Sunshine

Bees buzzing like a party song,
Flowers laughing, where they belong.
Sunshine spills like lemonade,
Dancing toes and a sun-warmed glade.

Picnics spread on plaid blankets wide,
Insects joining, they won't hide.
Sandwiches munch, and laughter rings,
Nature beckons and hilarity sings.

Ice cream drips down sticky hands,
As squirrels plot their snack demands.

The Last Dance of Joy

Twirling under the disco ball,
With mismatched socks, we have a ball.
Old records spin, the tunes are loud,
We dance like fools, oh, we are proud!

The floor's a mix of spills and cheer,
As silly moves draw everyone near.
A final spin, oh what a sight,
We twirl and laugh into the night.

Confetti falls like a party rain,
We hug the night without a gain.

Embraces Wrapped in Warmth

Big bear hugs, soft and tight,
As friends gather in sheer delight.
Hot cocoa flows like melted dreams,
Marshmallows bob, or so it seems.

A blanket fort made for kings and queens,
Where giggles blend with silly scenes.
Tales of mischief during the day,
In twilight glow, they all sway.

Home's a circus, and love's the ring,
Wrapped in warmth, oh what joy we bring!

The Last Frame of Us

In a world full of blame, we hid in plain sight,
Tickling each other till the morning light.
Every sigh, every giggle, a plot twist divine,
Chasing our shadows, you know, just like a vine.

With popcorn fights and a couch that won't budge,
Replaying our bloopers, we never do judge.
You trip on your dreams, I stumble on pride,
Yet hand in hand, we both glide with the tide.

The credits roll in; what a wild scene!
Fumbling the lines, just like a bad meme.
In frames of laughter, we dance through the end,
Life's a big joke, my forever friend.

So raise up your glass, here's to mischief and fun,
In the unrehearsed play, we've already won.
With every last giggle, we'll paint the sky bright,
Our ending's a banner, and oh, what a sight!

Timeless Serenades

We waltz through the years, through giggles and glee,
Singing off-key, just you and me.
With stars in our eyes and chaos in tow,
A karaoke duet, stealing each show.

Time clocks a timeout; we're dodging its tick,
With pranks of confetti and laughter's sweet trick.
Each serenade echoes, as funny dreams flow,
Like clowns in a circus, with nothing to show.

You trip on your thoughts; I barter my fate,
Trading our secrets at a comical rate.
In this timeless dance, with blunders we play,
We embrace every moment, come what may.

So here's to the laughter, the joy that we spread,
A symphony quirky that's never misled.
The world's our stage, and we're actors at heart,
In the funniest tale, we've both played a part.

A Journey Concluded in Bliss

We set out together with mismatched old shoes,
Wandering far down the roads we'd peruse.
With snacks uninvited and maps torn askew,
Every turn was a twist with not much to rue.

Our GPS broke, but we thrived on the thrill,
Making up landmarks, oh what a goodwill!
From mountains of laughter to valleys of glee,
We forged our own path, just you and me.

The finale approached, with jesters in tow,
With pies in our faces, it's quite the great show.
A grand silver lining on blunders galore,
So many odd moments we just can't ignore.

As we toast to the mischief, let echoes resound,
In this journey together, true love knows no bounds.
The bow is now taken, the curtain drawn tight,
What a hilarious saga, our ultimate flight.

Journeys with Open Hearts

In a car that won't start, we took our time,
Singing off-key, we thought it sublime.
Maps upside down, we lost our way,
But laughter and snacks made it a great day.

Through rain and mud, we danced with glee,
Wearing our woes like badges of spree.
A flat tire here, a coffee spill there,
Still, joy in the chaos, who could compare?

We talked of dreams under a bright moon,
Turning our struggles into a fun tune.
With each silly photo, we wrote our tale,
Learning that life's more than the perfect trail.

So here's to the paths both bumpy and wild,
Adventures we cherish, forever beguiled.
With hearts wide open and spirits so bright,
We'll keep on exploring, it feels just right.

The Bliss of Togetherness Unfolded

The kitchen's a mess, flour in our hair,
We made a soufflé, but it's not quite there.
With giggles and mishaps, we stir up delight,
Dinner for two? More like dinner fight!

The couch is our kingdom, snacks piled high,
Remote control battles — oh how we vie!
With movies that we both can't stand,
We hold each other tight, it's truly grand.

Board games turn frisky with rules all askew,
As we declare war, you're winning, it's true.
But in our hearts, we know we will share,
The laughter and mishaps that show we care.

So let's raise a toast to our curious plight,
Two silly souls making wrongs feel right.
In chaos we flourish, together we thrive,
Here's to the bliss where our love stays alive.

The Embrace of Time's Gentle Hand

Tick-tock, the clock knows just how to tease,
We're late to the party, oh what a breeze!
Wearing mismatched socks and our brightest grins,
We stroll through the door like we're kings and queens.

Each moment we fumble, we laugh it away,
As wine spills like stories we tell in dismay.
Old friends reminisce, with tales that entwine,
In the dance of our lives, oh how we shine.

The years roll along like a playful parade,
With sun-baked laughter, our fears we invade.
Perhaps we are older, or maybe just bold,
In this waltz of time, our love never grows old.

So here's to the joy of the years that we claim,
In the warmth of your smile, I'm glad I came.
With wrinkles and giggles, we take our stand,
Waltzing through time with our hearts hand in hand.

Whispers of Love in the Afterglow

As the day fades out, we giggle like spry,
Candlelit dinners with potato pie.
With crumbs on our laps and smiles on our face,
Whispers in twilight, we've found our place.

Stories from childhood, we swap with a grin,
Like how you once sprained your ankle in spin.
With laughter erupting and eyes all aglow,
Every silly moment adds love to our show.

Dreams drift like shadows, soft and serene,
In the quiet cocoon where our hearts convene.
With each little whisper, we grow and we play,
In this silly ballet, we dance through the fray.

So let's raise the curtain on this sweet refrain,
With love in our hearts, we'll dance in the rain.
In the twilight of togetherness, sweet and slow,
Our whispers of love will forever bestow.

The Sweetest Return

Home from work, they trod, quite spry,
With snacks in hand for hungry eyes.
Each jumped with joy, a grand surprise,
In mismatched socks, they danced nearby.

The cat on deck had stole the show,
In sunbeams warm, the laughter flowed.
They shared a joke, a silly throw,
And soon enough, all worries go.

With pie in hand, and hearts so bright,
They told tall tales with pure delight.
The night stretched on in pure twilight,
Until the stars winked "what a sight!"

As dreams take flight, they'll sing their song,
In every note, feel just how strong.
Together now, where they belong,
Hearts entwined in laughter, life's sweet throng.

Shores of Laughter

Upon the coast where seagulls play,
They built a castle made of hay.
With shovels tossed in a silly way,
They crafted smiles that brightened the day.

The tide rolled in to take a peek,
It giggled softly, finding its cheek.
Each wave whispered, "You're quite unique!"
Like ice cream cones, the joy was chic.

They splashed and dashed through sunlit beams,
In flip-flops lost, like silly dreams.
With every laugh, their friendship seems
To bloom like flowers in sunny themes.

As the sun dipped low in golden tides,
The group of friends, oh how they bide.
Through jokes and chips, their laughter rides,
In shores of joy where love abides.

Illuminated Paths

Through twilight trails, they wandered far,
With lanterns lit, like quirky stars.
Each twist and turn, a laughter bar,
Two friends together, sans any scars.

Beneath the moon, they played charades,
In silly hats, they tossed up aids.
With every misstep, giggles cascades,
Creating fun in friendly parades.

On winding roads, they chased the light,
With flickering smiles, their hearts took flight.
In generated joy, they felt so right,
And turned the mundane into pure delight.

Side by side as night cloaks all,
They shared their dreams, and dared to call.
With every chuckle, they'd stand tall,
In illuminated paths, they'd never fall.

A Flourish of Togetherness

In gardens bright with colors bold,
They planted seeds of stories told.
With every bloom, their friendship rolled,
In laughter shared, a warmth like gold.

With picnics set 'neath shady trees,
They feasted well, a playful tease.
Each silly dance swayed with the breeze,
Creating memories that always please.

As butterflies flitted overhead,
They painted dreams in hues of red.
With playful pranks, at dusk they fed
On cake and giggles, sweetly spread.

In every moment, joy is found,
With friendships forged in laughter's sound.
Together they'll spin tales profound,
In a flourish of togetherness, joy is crowned.

A Canvas of Cheer

With paintbrush in hand, I'll splash bright hues,
My cat leaps on canvas, I can't help but lose.
The sun sneezes golden, the clouds giggle loud,
As I dance with a paint pot, feeling quite proud.

Each stroke is a tickle, a laugh in disguise,
My friends all join in, and soon it's a prize.
A masterpiece formed with a splash and a grin,
Together we're painting the world with our kin.

The sky wears a smile, oh what a delight,
With every bright color, we banish the night.
Each laugh paints a story, each giggle a hue,
In this canvas of cheer, it's always brand new.

So bring me your laughter, your quirkiest tales,
We'll mix them with joy until happiness sails.
For here in this space, we're forever the same,
A joyful creation that plays in life's game.

Closing Chapter of Delight

The hero trips over a book with a smile,
Turns pages with zeal, oh it's quite the style.
Plot twists are waiting, let's turn on the light,
Each chapter a chuckle, oh what a sight!

The villain's a cat who just wants a warm lap,
While sidekicks keep asking, 'Hey, where's my nap?'
The jokes are all silly, the puns come in waves,
As laughter erupts, and the world just misbehaves.

The story winds down, the laughter still flows,
With each goofy gag, the heart truly knows.
The credits roll up, but we're still in our chairs,
Snickering and giggling, no one really cares.

So dear reader, fret not as we end this tale,
For happiness lingers, a shimmering trail.
As we close this book, know the joy will abide,
In every next chapter, let silliness ride.

The Bright Side of Dusk

As the sun does a jig and bids goodbye,
The fireflies gather, they buzz and they fly.
With twilight a canvas painted in jest,
We whisper our secrets and laugh with the best.

Shadows do waltz with a mischievous kick,
The moon pulls a prank, isn't that quite a trick?
We skip through the twilight with socks mismatched,
The bright side of dusk, oh how we've hatched!

The stars are confetti, thrown high in the sky,
As giggles erupt with each twinkle they spy.
A balloon floats by with a giggly face,
In this whimsical hour, we totally embrace.

So when day bids adieu in this playful way,
Remember to laugh as night makes its play.
With every sweet moment as twilight descends,
We find all the joy that the darkness extends.

A Serenade of Smiles

With silly serenades and laughs all around,
We sing to the moon, oh how we are bound.
Each note is a giggle, each chord a delight,
In this melody's grasp, everything's light.

The frogs join the chorus, a croak and a croon,
While fireflies shimmer like a bright summer moon.
Dancing on lawns, with shoes on our heads,
Our giggles erupt as we spin in our beds.

The whispers of joy float up with the breeze,
As the whole world chuckles beneath the tall trees.
A duet of laughter, so sweet to the ear,
In this serenade, we sing without fear.

So strum your own heartstrings, let chuckles resound,
As smiles fill the air, let our joy be profound.
For in every sweet note and each laugh we share,
We craft a life's symphony, happy and rare.

Laughter Echoes Through the Fields

In the meadow, cows wear hats,
Silly sheep play with acrobats.
The sun shines bright, birds sing tunes,
While daisies dance beneath the moons.

A pie that fell right on the ground,
A dog that barks with no good sound.
The butterflies wear shoes too small,
As laughter echoes, we have a ball.

The sky giggles as raindrops fall,
Just a tiny splash, not a waterfall.
Kids in puddles splash with glee,
Who knew mud could be so free?

In the fields where joy runs wild,
There's nothing quite like being a child.
With every chuckle, every cheer,
Laughter is the music we hold dear.

Where Stars Align and Hearts Connect

Under a sky of twinkling lights,
Two lost socks have epic fights.
A comet waves with a sassy blend,
Shooting stars agree, they won't offend.

Twirling in circles on the ground,
A dance-off starts without a sound.
Moonbeams winking as we align,
Dreams collide, it all feels fine.

Cats in spaceship hats launch snacks,
While teddy bears plan their midnight tracks.
The universe giggles, secrets unfold,
Every heart's story, hilariously told.

In this cosmic giggle fest,
We find the ones we love the best.
Friendship blooms beneath the sky,
Where laughter mingles and dreams fly high.

The Symphony of Sweet Goodbyes

The clock strikes twelve, a saxophone plays,
Goodbye to worries, here come the rays.
Balloons escape with a pop and a cheer,
As laughter lingers, happiness near.

The winking moon gives us a cue,
As we share stories, old and new.
Each hug a note in this sweet serenade,
Echoes of joy that will never fade.

Umbrellas flip in the sudden breeze,
While friends dance carefree, knees to knees.
With every giggle, a fond farewell,
In the symphony, we all excel.

When the last note fades, we won't forget,
The songs we wrote with no regret.
Goodbyes aren't sad, not in our hearts,
Just another tune where laughter starts.

Radiant Journeys, Endless Smiles

A train ride in a rainbow car,
Each station stop filled with candy bars.
With a giggle here and wink over there,
Laughter's our compass, guiding fair.

The sea turns blue, the sand is gold,
As stories of jokers and jesters unfold.
Beach towels fly like kites in the air,
While seagulls join in with a silly flair.

Adventure awaits on the horizon bright,
With every tickle, we take flight.
In sunlit laughter, we find our way,
Through radiant journeys, come what may.

Endless smiles, like bubbles in foam,
Every heartbeat shows we're home.
With friends beside us and giggles to share,
Life's the greatest adventure, without a care.

Golden Threads of Serendipity

In a twist of fate, they met,
A cat, a hat, a silly pet.
With laughter shared, they danced around,
In every smile, joy they found.

They tripped over dreams, how absurd,
A jumbled mix of silly words.
But in their chaos, light did bloom,
A garden grew from silly gloom.

Two clowns in life's grand parade,
With every blunder, love displayed.
Their joyful shouts filled the air,
A world transformed, with hearts laid bare.

And in each hiccup that they made,
A golden thread of joy conveyed.
Together they stitched a tale so bright,
Knit with laughter, their delight.

Tea and Tales by the Firelight

A kettle whistled, tales afloat,
With biscuits crumbled, laughter wrote.
Sipping tea, the stories spun,
Of mishaps, blunders, all in fun.

A squirrel danced with nimble toes,
While tea spilled out in sudden flows.
They laughed until their bellies hurt,
In cozy warmth, no ounce of curt.

The fire crackled, shadows played,
As silly noises always swayed.
A singed sock found in the heat,
Became a treasure, quite the feat.

With every cup that rose in cheer,
They toasted to friends who gathered near.
In laughter's glow, the night fell deep,
With tales of joy that never sleep.

A Canvas Painted in Gratitude

With splashes bright, the canvas sang,
In colors wild, the brushes sprang.
Each stroke a giggle, each hue a cheer,
A masterpiece born from laughter near.

A monkey swung with paint in hand,
Creating chaos, oh so grand.
Yet every drip turned out just right,
A joyful mess, a pure delight.

They painted hearts, and silly smiles,
Wove happiness across the miles.
With every color blending true,
Gratitude danced in every hue.

In this gallery of pure delight,
Where laughter painted day and night.
Their masterpiece, a joyous spree,
A testament to glee and glee.

The Promise of Tomorrow's Sun

The sun peeked out with a wink so sly,
A promise made to the blue sky.
With silly hats and dancing toes,
They welcomed laughter, as joy arose.

A jester's cap, a playful dance,
Each moment seized, a silly chance.
They spun around as if to say,
Tomorrow brings another play.

On rooftops high, the pigeons cooed,
As laughter swirled in every mood.
Together they'd chase the rising light,
Embracing each giggle, soft and bright.

With every dawn, a brand new jest,
In silliness, they found their rest.
A world awash in humor's run,
With every sunrise, the day's begun.

Beneath the Cherry Blossom

Beneath the tree we share a laugh,
Breezes tickle as we dance and chaff.
With petals falling, we take a chance,
Two silly hearts in a clumsy prance.

Squirrels giggle, watching from above,
We trip on roots, but it's all in love.
Ice cream drips on the sunny ground,
In this chaos, pure joy is found.

A kite gets stuck in our wacky hair,
But what do we care? We make a pair.
With each blunder, we just laugh more,
Here in the joy, who could ask for more?

As the sun sets, we clink our drinks,
Life's a comedy, or so it thinks.
Under cherry blooms, we'll shimmy and sway,
A fool's paradise, forever we'll play.

The Morning After Happiness

Waking up to chaotic bliss,
We giggle at each forgetful kiss.
The toaster burnt but we're not blue,
Breakfast for champions, or was that a stew?

Mismatch socks and a coffee stain,
Dancing in pajamas, this is our gain.
Hair like a bird's nest, we strut outside,
What's left for shame? We take it in stride.

Neighbors peek through their window blinds,
At our antics, they chuckle, it shines.
Living the dream with a dash of absurd,
Each little mishap, laughter's the word.

With each little step, we're a clumsy pair,
Chasing the sun with no hint of care.
The morning light smiles as if to say,
Life's an odd theater, come laugh and play!

Where Wishes Come True

At the fountain, we tossed our coins,
Hoping for magic, embracing our joys.
But what sprouted from the depths below,
A fish in a tux, put on quite a show.

We laughed so hard the onlookers stared,
As he juggled bubbles, completely bared.
One popped with a splat, we squealed with glee,
In the world of wishes, we'll never decree.

Dreams in our pockets, we danced down the lane,
While ducks quacked tunes, they brought the rain.
Umbrellas flipped, we spun and we swirled,
In our little chaos, pure joy is unfurled.

With wishes ungranted yet spirits so bright,
We twirled like dervishes, lighting the night.
In this circus of wishes, we'll always stay true,
Chasing the laughter where dreams come anew.

Heartbeats of Jubilation

In a world of giggles, our hearts collide,
We skip like stones, with mischief as our guide.
A rubber chicken, our secret weapon,
With each squawk of laughter, anxiety's leaven.

We wear silly hats that defy the rules,
Turning stares into smiles, forget the fools.
With a hop and a wiggle, we rule the street,
Two jesters united, oh what a feat!

A bubble wrap path that pops with delight,
Each step like a dance, filled with pure light.
We race the clouds with our inner children,
Finding joy in the fog, where laughter is hidden.

As the sun waves its golden goodbye,
We leap to the stars, our spirits can fly.
Heartbeats of jubilation, an echoing cheer,
In our funny adventure, happiness is near.

Whispers of Joy Beneath Moonlit Skies

The stars blink down with glee,
As cats dance in a tree.
The moon chuckles bright and loud,
While crickets form a cheering crowd.

With laughter echoing in the air,
We twirl beneath without a care.
A squirrel joins with a wiggly jig,
Oh, life is one great cherry gig!

The Dance of Dreams Fulfilled

In slippers soft, we glide and sway,
As dreams return to dance today.
A monkey swings with style and flair,
While giggles float like bubbles rare.

The table's set for cake and fun,
Where laughter's served, we're never done.
With frosting smiles on every slice,
Who knew that joy could taste so nice?

Sunflowers in Full Bloom

Sunflowers tickle in the breeze,
Their heads nodding with such ease.
Bees buzz by, all dressed in black,
While butterflies go on the snack track.

A sunflower wore a goofy hat,
He flashed a smile; how about that?
The garden's filled with silly fun,
Where every petal's like a pun!

Embracing the Gentle Breeze

The breeze plays tag, it sneaks and darts,
It lifts our spirits, light as tarts.
With every twist, the world sings bright,
As leaves do cha-chas in delight.

We laugh and spin like tops on fire,
Our silly dance, each step, a choir.
With breezy giggles wrapped around,
In joy's embrace, we're laughter-bound!

A Candle Lit in Joy

In the dark, we cheer and sing,
With cake and laughter, joy takes wing.
The candles flicker, each a spark,
A dance of dreams, we leave our mark.

With silly hats and faces bright,
In every hug, the world feels right.
We toast to moments, shared and true,
A circus show, with a joyful crew.

As we blow out each glowing flame,
The wish we share, a playful game.
We'll take this night and hold it tight,
With every chuckle, hearts feel light.

So let's keep dancing, come what may,
In our own world, we love to play.
For every giggle, for every cheer,
This joyful night, we hold so dear.

Kaleidoscope of Promises

Twists and turns in bright array,
We laugh at life, come what may.
Each promise shines like a wild dream,
In this jigsaw world, we're a team.

Colors blend like friends in hugs,
Together we share our sassy shrugs.
From sunny days to rainy skies,
We trade our jokes and silly lies.

A flip of fate, and there we go,
With a wink and a giggle, steal the show.
The stories spin, a whimsy fad,
In this lively dance, we're never sad.

So let's shake hands with fate's old game,
In a whirlwind joy, we claim our name.
With laughter bright, we'll spin around,
A kaleidoscope of love we've found.

Fonts of Friendship

In the font of joy, we play and rhyme,
With every word, we steal some time.
Bold letters leap, a goofy spree,
In script and curve, we feel so free.

Comic Sans in swirls of cheer,
Makes every joke seem crystal clear.
We scribble dreams with sharpie pens,
In the book of life, we're family friends.

Serif tales with laughter keen,
Every story's better when we glean.
With shaded smiles and playful tease,
Together we write, adventures please.

So let's print moments, crisp and bright,
In the font of friendship, all feels right.
Doodles of joy fill every page,
In the workshop of life, we take the stage.

Echoes of Our Laughter

In the halls where giggles play,
Echoes bounce in the silliest way.
We chase the echoes, twirling free,
In the symphony of you and me.

Let the chuckles spill and soar,
In this joyful sound, we crave more.
Slapstick moments fill our days,
In the laughter loop, we weave our ways.

Tickles of joy, a ripple wide,
With every joke, we're filled with pride.
We dance along the whispered sounds,
In laughter's rhythm, love abounds.

So join the chorus, loud and bright,
In the echoes of our laughter's flight.
With every giggle, we'll raise a cheer,
This joyous melody we hold so dear.

A Celebration of Us

In a world full of chaos, we dance in delight,
With socks that don't match, we twirl through the night.
A cake made of laughter, with sprinkles of cheer,
We celebrate moments that bring us good beer.

Jumping in puddles, wearing our best frowns,
Turning sad faces to giggles and crowns.
Each mishap a treasure, each stumble a song,
In this circus of life, we always belong.

Crystal Clear Reflections

Looking in mirrors that rattle and shake,
We giggle at faces that make the ground quake.
With hair like a tornado, and socks full of fluff,
Life's silly reflections remind us to bluff.

We ponder the future, with winks and a grin,
Dancing to tunes that make no sense within.
In the pool of our laughter, we dive and we splash,
Crystal clear outlooks that turn frowns to a dash.

A Letter from Tomorrow

Dear future me, I hope you're in style,
With shoes that don't squeak and a reason to smile.
I sent you some cookies, and one funny joke,
To lighten your burdens and keep you bespoke.

Remember to wiggle, and never to pout,
For every small mishap's what life's all about.
I've packed up some giggles for journeys ahead,
And if you find trouble, just dance instead!

The Bouquet of Today

I picked a bouquet of moments so bright,
With petals of laughter that take off in flight.
Each flower a memory, a giggle, a cheer,
Together we bloom, with nothing to fear.

The daisies of nonsense in sunlight so gold,
Mixed in with the pansies that never grow old.
With each little chuckle, I gather in joy,
This bouquet of today is a gift to deploy.

The Final Embrace

In a world where chaos reigns,
A cat wears socks and walks on chains.
The birds all laugh, they crack a grin,
As the dog does backflips, let the fun begin!

The trees are dancing, swaying free,
A squirrel's planning a jubilee!
The sun paints stripes upon the grass,
While neighbors gossip as their pets all sass.

With dancing shoes, the rabbits prance,
Every bunny's ready for a chance!
They twirl around the playful breeze,
As giggles fill the air, with ease!

When night falls gently, hearts still race,
A sleepy smile upon each face.
With laughter echoing through the park,
The final hug ignites a spark.

Radiant Revelations

A llama shows up in a bright pink hat,
With glasses perched upon her fat.
She twirls around with such delight,
As cupcakes dance around at night.

The stars all wink with silly glee,
While moonbeams shine on all that's free.
A frog begins to serenade,
The fireflies join, unafraid.

With whispers sweet and jokes galore,
The night unfolds with a silly roar.
A hedgehog juggles, just for fun,
Chasing shadows 'til they run.

When morning comes, we raise a toast,
To all the moments we love the most.
With hugs and giggles, we take our chance,
In this grand dance, we all advance!

Harmony's Arrival

The circus comes to town today,
With elephants that dance and sway.
A jester's tricks make everyone laugh,
While children play on the grassy path.

A parade of colors fills the streets,
With marching bands and happy beats.
A cat in shoes moves to the sound,
As joyful chaos spreads around.

With popcorn flying in the air,
And laughter echoing everywhere.
The sun shines bright, the skies are blue,
While silly hats adorn the crew.

When the day ends with fireworks bright,
Joyful hearts embrace the night.
With smiles wide, we wave goodbye,
Ready to laugh, as time flies by.

The Sweetest Farewell

As we gather for one last cheer,
The garden's filled with joy and beer.
With funny hats atop our heads,
We reminisce the tales we've spread.

A parrot squawks a funny tune,
While dancing under the glowing moon.
The neighbors peek with curious glee,
As we toast to memories, wild and free.

The cake is large, too big to hold,
With sprinkles bursting, bright and bold.
We share our laughs; we share the cake,
And bid adieu to all we make.

With arms wide open, we say farewell,
To all the stories we'll retell.
With silly grins and hearts so bright,
We'll find our way back, come morning light.

The Tranquil Path Forward

On a road paved with jelly beans,
We skip and hop like silly teens.
With every step, we break into song,
Dancing like we can't do wrong.

The trees join in with a creaky sway,
Singing tunes of a bright new day.
Each giggle echoes through the breeze,
Tickling our ears like playful tease.

A squirrel strikes poses, a true ballet,
He twirls in joy, come what may.
With laughter popping like corn on fire,
We're racing ahead, chasing our desire.

The sun smiles wide, a wink from afar,
Guiding us home like a bright North Star.
Together we journey, never alone,
Marching onward to our own happy tone.

The Essence of Together

Hand in hand through thick and thin,
With a wink, you'd say, 'Let the fun begin!'
Sharing stories like pies to share,
Crusty and flaky, but full of care.

In a world where clowns wear frowns,
We flip their woes and turn them upside down.
With pie fights and silly hats galore,
We fill our days with laughter's roar.

Dancing over puddles, making big splashes,
Wearing our joy like glittering sashes.
With every chuckle, our hearts grow fonder,
Creating a bond like the stars grow yonder.

Every joke is a thread in our weave,
Knitting memories too good to leave.
Together we shine, a luminous pair,
In the garden of giggles, we light up the air.

A Harvest of Laughter

In fields where the giggles grow tall and sweet,
We gather our joy, a delightful treat.
With baskets made of sunshine and cheer,
We pick up the laughter that draws us near.

Each chuckle's a berry, ripe for the plucking,
Squirrels are cheering, the world is trucking.
The daisies dance as the wind gives a twirl,
While we toss our worries and let laughter whirl.

When life hands us lemons, we make lemonade,
With sprinkles of joy, like a fun charade.
We sip from our cups filled with giggly glee,
Creating a feast where we laugh 'til we pee!

A harvest of stories, sweet and sublime,
Every goofy moment's worth savoring time.
With friends by our side in this silly spree,
We cultivate happiness, wild and free.

Glimmers of Hope

In the corners of chaos, we find little lights,
Sparkling like fireflies on warm summer nights.
With jokes that land like a pillow fight,
We chase away shadows, banish the fright.

A world made of giggles is a glorious sight,
Where the clouds wear sunglasses, oh so bright!
With laughter as fuel, we zoom through the day,
Turning troubles to wobbles in a silly ballet.

Each riddle unraveled brings shouts of delight,
Like a pie in the face at the end of a fight.
In the tapestry of life, we stitch with a grin,
Finding joy in the mess, and letting love in.

So when moments go sideways, don't pout and mope,
Just look for the glimmers, the sparkles of hope.
With hearts full of laughter, we forever will soar,
Crafting a symphony that's never a bore.

Unveiled Secrets in the Heart's Archive

In the attic of my chest, truths unfold,
Dust bunnies whisper, tales of old.
Love notes hid in socks, such a find,
Each laugh a gem, scattered in the mind.

Socks that tango and shirts that sing,
All my secrets, doing their thing.
A dance of memories, a pie in the face,
Who knew chaos could find such a place?

The clock strikes twelve, the party's a roar,
Finding treasures behind every door.
With pillows that giggle and blankets that cheer,
Every stumble leads to joy, my dear!

So here I unveil, with a wink and a grin,
The heart's archive where the fun begins.
Each hidden delight, a pudding surprise,
Life's funny twists brought tears to our eyes.

Cherished Moments on a Woven Path

On this carpet of gold, I dance with my feet,
Twists and turns make the journey sweet.
A tumble here, a giggle there,
Laughter wraps me up in delightful despair.

Chasing rainbows while wearing mismatched shoes,
Life's whimsical moments, can't lose or snooze.
Pixie dust sprinkled in every misstep,
Magical mishaps, oh what a rep!

The squirrels watch closely, taking their notes,
As I trip over dreams, igniting my hopes.
With each little stumble, I rise even taller,
Celebrating the fall, my laughter's the caller.

With smiles like confetti and love in a jar,
These cherished moments will follow me far.
Woven paths lead to joy, a colorful race,
Every twist of fate brings a new embrace.

The Lightness of Being, Tender and True

Floating like bubbles, we drift through the day,
Lives intertwined in a charming ballet.
With jests that tickle and quirks that shine,
We dance on the breeze, sipping sweet wine.

The moon winks at us with a knowing grin,
As we tumble and spin, letting lightness in.
Whimsical wishes, held close to the heart,
Each laugh a balloon, we'll never depart.

In gardens of giggles, flowers bloom bright,
Whispered secrets under the starlit night.
Running barefoot through puddles of bliss,
An umbrella of joy, it's hard to miss.

With each little quirk, our hearts bloom anew,
Creating a tapestry in shades of true.
And when the sun sets, we'll still be around,
Dancing in dreams where joy can abound.

Kaleidoscope of Grateful Hearts

In a twist of fate, our hearts find their glee,
Colors collide in pure jubilee.
Grateful for tickles and sprinkles of cheer,
We paint our days bright, with laughter sincere.

With hats on our heads, we pursue silly dreams,
Like cats on skateboards, we burst at the seams.
Every moment a canvas, each laugh a sweet brush,
In a world made of giggles, we're never in a rush.

Open your heart, let the joy overflow,
In this kaleidoscope life, watch the colors glow.
Each twist and each turn, we laugh hand in hand,
Together creating our whimsical land.

So gather your giggles and share them wide,
In this colorful journey, let love be your guide.
Kaleidoscope hearts make the best of the art,
In the tapestry woven, we'll never fall apart.

Golden Circles of Trust

In a park where ducks all quack,
We share our sandwiches, no lack.
Laughter echoes, fills the air,
With mustard stains, we wear our flair.

Chasing squirrels, we make a dash,
Falling over, what a crash!
But in our tangle, joy remains,
In golden circles, free of chains.

A game of tag, a silly fight,
We tumble down, what pure delight!
Giggles echo into the dusk,
In our little world, it's always a must.

So hand in hand, we stroll around,
With silly hats, we dance, profound.
In this circle, trust prevails,
Where every breeze tells happy tales.

The Radiance of Togetherness

In our fort made of old sheets,
Giggles rise like tasty treats.
We sip our juice, the sun's bright glare,
In laughter's warmth, we do not care.

With borrowed hats and mismatched socks,
We dance around like crazy clocks.
Each twirl's a story, joyful and bold,
In vibrant hues of tales retold.

Building castles from the sand,
With sticky fingers, all unplanned.
Every sand grain holds our dreams,
In this world, laughter beams.

So here's to us, misfits at heart,
In this imperfect, perfect part.
Where every moment radiates,
Togetherness—it never waits.

Threads of Delight

With crayons drawn, we start to weave,
A tapestry of tricks, believe!
Red and blue, they twist and twine,
In playful chaos, hearts align.

A jump rope game, I miss my skip,
Just one more try, I barely trip.
But laughter spins in every fall,
With tangled threads, we've got it all.

In sewing mishaps, patches bright,
We craft our joys, all day and night.
Each snip and stitch, a giggle shared,
In threads of delight, we are ensnared.

So let's unite in thread and hue,
Creating moments, ever new.
As nimble fingers dance with glee,
In this quilted joy, we are free.

Moments that Sparkle

With glitter glue and crafty dreams,
We craft our joy in giggly beams.
A paper plane that flies too low,
Yet every crash brings more to show.

In backyard games under the sun,
We race our shadows, oh, what fun!
With hopscotch paths and silly songs,
Each moment dances, it belongs.

Caught in sunshine, we sip our juice,
Mixing flavors, one wild moose!
Stains on shirts, we wear with pride,
In laughter's glow, we do not hide.

So here's to life, its twists and turns,
In every sparkle, the heart still yearns.
We'll cherish moments, big and small,
In joyful chaos, we'll have it all.

Notes of Serenity in Life's Ballad

In a world where socks don't match,
We dance like no one's watching,
With mismatched shoes, we take a chance,
Each step a giggle, our hearts are launching.

The cat steals the spotlight, it's true,
While we twist and twirl in delight,
With pancakes stacked high in a queue,
Our laughter echoes through the night.

Spilled drinks become our finest art,
Champagne wishes on a soda budget,
Yet every flop is a work of heart,
In our cabinet of memories, we trudge.

The sun sets low, a wink from the sky,
As we toast to our funny misleads,
With balloons that soar and a joyous sigh,
Life's quirks are just what our spirit needs.

The Last Page of a Beautiful Story

As the final chapter draws near,
We chuckle at plot twists galore,
A character sneezes, while we cheer,
What's life without laughter to explore?

The villain trips on their own cape,
With every blunder, we break into fits,
Our hearts feel light, no room for drape,
In this tale, humor tightly knits.

We gather 'round at the book's end,
With snacks and tales that enlarge our glee,
Every turn in the tale, we recommend,
For laughter, dear friends, is the best spree!

So let's close this book, though it's not sad,
With smiles that linger, it's quite good,
In memory, we hold what we've had,
A story well told in our cheerful neighborhood.

Whispers of Joy

In a garden where daisies play tout,
We dance with butterflies, carefree and spry,
With whispers of joy that twirl about,
Victory is sweet, with donuts nearby.

The squirrel steals a nut, oh what a scene!
Underneath the old oak, we share our stash,
With giggles and crumbs, we reign supreme,
Our picnic erupts in a pie-filled clash.

Every hiccup a song, every mistake a dance,
We'll twirl 'round the sun, our laughter their guide,
Though life can be silly, we'll always enhance,
With each little joy, we won't try to hide.

So let's chase the rainbows, skip every rock,
With joy as our whisper and laughter our crack,
In this silly world, we'll break every clock,
For every moment shared, we've no reason to lack.

The Last Note of Laughter

As the curtain falls on our funny play,
We bow with grins, our hearts in a race,
With inside jokes we'll replay all day,
Each snicker a memory, laughter's embrace.

The punchline lands like a well-thrown pie,
Audience still chuckles, all hold their breath,
The mustard jar lid, a comic goodbye,
With joy in our hearts, we laugh at our depth.

The lights dim low, the spotlight fades,
Yet echoes remain of our funny parade,
In every cackle and whimsical phrase,
We'll cherish each giggle as history's trade.

As we exit stage left, leaving with cheer,
Our final act ends in a thunderous roar,
With humor leading, we've nothing to fear,
In the book of our lives, laughter's encore.

The Blossoms of Our Story

In a garden of giggles, we danced with glee,
Chasing butterflies, just you and me.
With cupcakes and laughter, we filled our days,
Turning mundane moments into bright arrays.

The sun wore a hat, all jaunty and round,
While we tumbled over, feet barely on ground.
Each misstep a treasure, each fall a delight,
Our bliss was a riddle, wrapped up tight.

A dog with a bowtie joined in the game,
He stole all the snacks, but who could blame?
We laughed and we cried, through each little spree,
Our story unfurled like a grand jubilee.

Through puddles we splashed, like kids on the spree,
Sprinkled with joy, just as it should be.
With a wink and a grin, we danced under stars,
In this sweet little tale, there are no cold jars.

The Sweet Remembering

With ice cream in hand, we strolled down the lane,
Recalling the awkward moments, quite plain.
You slipped on a banana, I fell in a stream,
Yet we laughed it off, caught up in the dream.

Whispers of mischief filled each frosty night,
As we plotted our pranks, every one a delight.
Silly hats and wigs were our chosen attire,
Our antics would surely set the town afire.

Remember when we dressed like superheroes bold?
In capes made of sheets, our secrets we told.
We zoomed through the park with grace only obscure,
Fearless and funny, of that we were sure.

Now as we share tales over cups of hot cheer,
We laugh till we stumble, no hint of a tear.
In a world so weird, we found our own song,
Forever in joy, where our hearts belong.

Serenade to Forever

Under a moonbeam, we crafted our tune,
Singing off-key beneath the round moon.
With spoons as guitars, we strummed through the night,
Pajamas and laughter were our pure delight.

The squirrels were our audience, quite stunned and amazed,
As we belted out ballads, utterly crazed.
Our melody wobbled, but spirits did soar,
In this charming chaos, we wanted more.

With every off-note, our hearts held their ground,
A symphony silly, a connection profound.
We twirled with the shadows, our steps all askew,
The world turned to giggles as the stars twinkled too.

So here in this moment, my dear, we will stay,
Embracing the quirks in our own special way.
Our serenade lingers, with humor we sprinkle,
Forever in laughter, where joy's never simple.

The Final Bow

As curtains draw close on our playful parade,
We take our last bow in the grand masquerade.
With confetti in hair and smiles smeared wide,
We journeyed together, side by side.

The stage was our playground, where laughter ran free,
We tumbled through skits, just as it should be.
With wigs askew and a pie in the face,
Our antics brought joy like a warm, sweet embrace.

Each blooper a treasure, each flub a delight,
Together we shone, under soft golden light.
In puns and in giggles, our hearts sang out loud,
Celebrating our journey with laughter, so proud.

So here's to the memories, both silly and true,
In the end it was laughter, just me and you.
With a wink and a wave, our curtain does fall,
In the theater of life, we giggled through all.

Echoes of Serenity

In a world of socks, mismatched and bright,
Dancing with glee, oh what a sight!
The cat's on a mission, it's true and sincere,
Chasing her tail, without any fear.

A sandwich takes flight, with mustard and cheese,
Floating away on a breeze with such ease.
The birds in the trees giggle and tweet,
As pickles join forces with grapes for a treat.

The clock cracks a joke, we all burst in glee,
"Time flies, but never quite just like me!"
With balloons all around, we laugh 'til we cry,
In this zany land, we'll reach for the sky.

The suns all wear sunglasses, dancing on high,
While clouds play the drums, as the raindrops fly.
Every moment a sketch in this colorful draw,
We spin 'round the world in happy uproar.

The Happy Horizon

On sunny days full of mischievous cheer,
The ice cream truck plays, ringing loud and clear.
Squirrels wear hats, having picnics galore,
Sharing their acorns, always asking for more.

A cow in a tutu dances by the fence,
While chickens tell jokes that defy common sense.
The sun winks at flowers, they start to bloom,
As laughter erupts from the old garden gnome.

The breeze whispers secrets to the rustling leaves,
And the bees in this place have their own little thieves.
With honey on toast, we munch side by side,
In this quirky wonder, let happiness guide.

Pirates with sandwiches sail in the sky,
Their ship is a toaster, oh me, oh my!
With forks as their cannons, they battle with cake,
The joy of this realm is too good to fake.

Dreams Woven in Gold

Napping on clouds, as soft as can be,
A snail tells a tale of ten cups of tea.
The sun paints the world with a silly grin,
While raindrops tap dance, let the fun begin!

A rabbit with glasses reads books on a train,
While jellybeans rattle in the sky, sans rain.
A parade of the odd, let's all join the show,
As vegetables tango, and dance to and fro.

The moon wears a hat, twinkling with pride,
As shadows play games, and night is our guide.
We'll create funny stories on this golden path,
Doing cartwheels of joy, no time for the math.

Under the stars, our giggles take flight,
With marshmallows bouncing through the magical night.
And just like that, with a flip and a toss,
We find in our hearts, laughter never gets lost.

Laughter Beneath the Stars

The stars are all chuckling, not one is aloof,
As socks fly like rockets, defying the roof.
An octopus juggles, it's quite a weird sight,
While crickets form bands to play through the night.

A turtle in shades rides a bike down the lane,
With ice cream all over its shell, what a gain!
While fireflies twinkle, they make quite a scene,
As laughter erupts to the beat of a dream.

Balloons paint the sky in colors so grand,
As penguins on roller skates take a stand.
Champagne made of bubbles pops all around,
As joy paints the canvas, so richly profound.

So let's spin in circles beneath the night sky,
With winks and with giggles, oh me, oh my!
In this carnival of dreams, forever we'll stay,
With laughter our compass, we'll dance 'til the day.

Harmonies of Laughter in Time's Embrace

In a world of giggles, we dance all day,
With silly hats and shoes that sway.
Tickling time with every laugh,
Our joy's the map, and fun's the path.

Bouncing like bubbles in sunshine's glow,
We trip on laughter, it's quite the show!
Each chuckle a spark, we light the night,
With whimsy and glee, everything feels right.

Through jumbled words and playful pranks,
We raise our mugs, give heartfelt thanks.
For every blunder, there's joy to find,
In the circus of life where we unwind.

So let's toast to moments that make us sing,
With half-baked ideas, let the giggles ring.
As we sway in sync, let the laughter flow,
Holding close our warmth, in this perfect show.

A Garden of Wishes Blooming Bright

In a garden where dreams sprout like weeds,
We plant our laughter, and pull out the creeds.
With dandelion wishes, we toss in the air,
Each giggle that sprouts grows everywhere.

Petals of joy in colors so bold,
We water them daily with stories retold.
With honeyed humor, we tend to the scene,
Where smiles are flowers, lush and serene.

Amongst the sunflowers, we play hide and seek,
Chasing the shadows, now cheek to cheek.
Pollinating dreams with jokes we unfold,
In this garden of wishes, our hearts never cold.

As the bees buzz along to our silly refrain,
We dance through the blooms, joy's sweet gain.
With laughter as sunshine, our hearts take flight,
In this cheery patch where everything's bright.

Beneath the Canopy of Stardust

Beneath the twinkling canopy of night,
We trip over stardust, oh what a sight!
With wishes on lips and giggles on breeze,
The universe chuckles, doused in tease.

We dance on the clouds, with flares in our eyes,
Chasing our laughter, reaching for skies.
A lighthearted waltz through the cosmic ballet,
Where stars smirk and wink in their own funny way.

With moonbeams as shoes, let's boogie and sway,
Each tumble a treasure, not just child's play.
In this stellar playground, our joy takes flight,
Lost in the rhythm of a whimsical night.

So let's toast to the heavens, our spirits so high,
With stardust confetti, we'll reach for the sky.
Laughter ringing clearly, like bells in the dark,
In this cosmic adventure, we ignite the spark.

Reflection of Joy on Still Waters

On a lake of giggles where ripples create,
We row our boats, oh isn't it great?
Paddling through chuckles, a splash here and there,
As laughter echoes, we chase without care.

With every splash, a memory forms,
In the mirror of water, the laughter transforms.
Fish flip and dive, doing their dance,
While ducks quack along, joining the prance.

The sun throws its sparkles, gold on the waves,
Each twinkle a joke that the water behaves.
We toast with our paddles, let the fun soar,
In this calm oasis, who could ask for more?

So let's cast our wishes, as we float with ease,
In this silly dreamscape, where hearts can seize.
With joy as our anchor, we sail and sing,
In reflections of laughter, what bliss they bring.

A Garden of Contented Hearts

In a garden where giggles bloom,
Sunshine dances, dispelling gloom.
Bumblebees wear tiny hats,
And daisies chat with the acrobatic cats.

Every flower cracks a joke,
Even the bushes join the poke.
Worms wiggle in delightful cheer,
While butterflies toast with ginger beer.

The rosebuds share tales of delight,
As ladybugs play hide and seek at night.
The sun sets low, painting the sky,
While garden critters wish you goodbye.

In this realm where laughter thrives,
Even the chickens wear party vibes.
So come and stay, don't be shy,
In this garden, we touch the sky!

The Final Piece of the Puzzle

In a jigsaw world where laughter fits,
Each piece giggles, and nobody quits.
Some are odd, with colors bright,
While others grumble but end in delight.

A corner piece dreamed of being straight,
Looked at edges, thought, 'This is fate!'
All mixed up, they shook with glee,
Pretending to be a trendy tee.

The center piece claimed it knew best,
While a stray bit said, 'Take a rest!'
Together they danced, twirled around,
Finding joy in their shapes unbound.

At last, the last piece came in with flair,
And completion sparked a party rare.
Laughter erupted, it was wild!
Even the box joined, feeling like a child!

Reflections of Euphoria

In a realm of giggles, light does beam,
Mirrors shimmer with a joyous dream.
Laughing reflections, all around,
Chasing silliness where glee is found.

A pirate's patch found a wink,
As fairies danced and began to think.
Every glance sparked a playful cheer,
While silly sounds filled every ear.

One mirror whispered jokes at dusk,
While others giggled, in sparkle and musk.
"Look at my hair!" a cat did shout,
"Where's my tail?" became a playful pout.

With cheers and chuckles filling the space,
Euphoria echoed in every face.
Reflect on joy; let your heart sing,
In this magic, we find our spring!

Wings of Cheer

On wings of laughter, they take to flight,
Silly birds sparkle, day and night.
With feathery hats and shoes so bright,
They swirl and twirl in sheer delight.

One bird sang of a marmalade cat,
While all the rest giggled, 'Imagine that!'
They flew so high on a bubble's grace,
And painted the clouds with a smiley face.

A worm waved a flag, said, "Look at me!"
While ants lined up for a grand jubilee.
Feathers ruffled in splendid swoops,
As they performed for giggling groups.

The sun dipped low, their dance winding down,
With every cheer, they wore a crown.
In this sky where joy takes charge,
Life is a joke, and we laugh at large!

Stars Aligned for Us

In a dance of fate, we took a chance,
With mismatched socks and a silly stance.
Laughter echoed, the skies turned bright,
Our hearts twirled in the gleeful night.

We tripped on dreams, but oh, what fun!
Chasing rainbows, we always run.
Starry eyes and ridiculous grins,
Together we lose, yet always win.

The moon winked down, a cheeky tease,
We made wishes with the greatest ease.
On cloud nine, in pajamas we'd lay,
In goofy bliss, we fondly stay.

With silly songs and dances galore,
What's life without a little uproar?
As stars aligned, we knew it's true,
This wild ride's made for me and you.

Treasures of a Grateful Heart

With spoons for hats and pies on our heads,
We counted blessings, despite our dreads.
A treasure map with X on our chest,
Eating cookies, we felt so blessed.

Gratitude flows like spilled milk, you see,
In laughter's embrace, we dance wild and free.
A heart full of gold and some chocolate too,
We find joy in each bizarre point of view.

In puddles we splash, ignoring the rain,
With friends by our side, we share all the gain.
Every little quirk, we treasure with glee,
In this quirky world, it's just you and me.

Through chaotic days and mishaps galore,
We gather our treasures, each moment we score.
So here's to the laughter, the joy that we start,
In this goofy life, I treasure your heart.

All Roads Lead to Joy

We wandered in circles, a marvelous feat,
Lost in thoughts of something to eat.
Each road we traveled was utterly wrong,
But we laughed it off, singing our song.

Detours became our dancing spots,
Turning our blunders into joyful lots.
Through winding paths, we laughed and played,
Making memories that never fade.

With ice cream stains and a dog on a leash,
Our goofy adventures never cease.
Every misstep brought giggles galore,
In this wacky journey, we always want more.

All roads may twist, but we don't mind,
For joy is the treasure that we all find.
As we cruise through life, hand in hand,
We laugh our way through this wobbly land.

Gifts of a Grateful Soul

With silly socks and mismatched shoes,
We count our gifts, it's how we choose.
From belly laughs to hugs so tight,
Each day's a victory, pure delight.

Signed and sealed with a goofy grin,
Wrapped in laughter, that's where we win.
The gift of a friend, a silly joke,
In gratitude's glow, our hearts we stoke.

With every mishap, we learn and cheer,
Collecting moments we hold so dear.
From the mundane to the extraordinary,
Each gift reveals our secret story.

So here's to the quirks that make us glow,
To the laughter that sparkles, helping us grow.
In the gift of love, in all that we share,
The treasures of life are beyond compare.

From Shadows to Sunbeams

Woke up late, my hair a mess,
Coffee spilled, oh what a stress.
Tripped on shoes, and down I went,
But a laugh crept out, my worries spent.

Sun peeked in, it kissed my cheek,
Life's just funny, so to speak.
From grumpy frowns to giggles bright,
Every blunder feels just right.

Friends arrive, with jokes in hand,
Together we stumble, it's all so grand.
Cake that falls, oh what a shame,
We'll just eat it all, it's still the same!

So here's to life, with quirks and twists,
Finding joy where you least expect it.
In every blunder, we find our cheer,
A perfect laugh, let's give a cheer!

A Tapestry Woven in Warmth

Stitches laughing with every thread,
Quilting memories, where's the dread?
Patterned chaos all around,
Giggling friends, our love profound.

Hot glue gun scars from arts and crafts,
Sticky fingers and joyful laughs.
Laughter echoes through the room,
As we create, all worries loom.

Songs are sung, off-key delight,
Dancing shadows in the moonlight.
Each misstep a reason for glee,
In this tapestry, we are free.

So let's weave on, with threads so bright,
In warmth and joy, we'll take our flight.
With every stitch, a tale we tell,
Life's crooked path, we know it well.

Chasing the Elysian Dream

Running fast through fields of glee,
On roller skates, not meant to be!
Tripped on daisies, who'd have thought?
Elysian laughs are what we caught.

Clouds are fluff, and sun's a game,
Chasing bubbles, who's to blame?
Each pop a giggle, joy's aroma,
Skipping through like sweet balona.

Caught a butterfly, well, not quite,
It fluttered off, oh what a sight!
But in the chase, the fun is spun,
Elysian heights, oh what a run!

So here we hop, with silly grace,
Joy in our hearts, we find our place.
Chasing dreams, oh what a scheme,
Life, it seems, is one big dream!

Embers of Happiness in Quiet Nights

Stars above, they blink and wink,
Peeking through, as we all think.
S'mores are sticky, firelight glows,
Laughter bubbles, as friendship grows.

In quiet nights, our secrets flow,
Ghost stories told, not one is slow.
Marshmallow wars take the crown,
Covered in goo, we laugh and frown.

Even the crickets join the spree,
Chirping along, come sing with me!
Embers flicker, this fire's warm,
Through every mishap, a friendship's charm.

With sleepy heads, we start to drift,
In every chuckle, life's little gift.
Under the stars, we've found our light,
In soft whispers, a perfect night!

Hues of Happiness

In a world where misfits smile,
A cat in a hat rode a mile.
Zebras painted in bright neon stripes,
Dance with unicorns, oh what types!

Jellybeans rain from a clear blue sky,
Silly monkeys teach us to fly.
Sippin' lemonade from a shoe,
Life's a party, who knew?

An octopus plays the accordion,
While flamingos groove in their union.
Spinning top hats and shuffleboard,
Their laughter is the sweetest reward.

At the end of the road, we cheer,
With bubbles popping, never fear!
A tickle fight with fate's own jest,
In this crazy land, we are blessed!

The Final Dawn

Roosters in sunglasses strut with pride,
As chaos joins the morning tide.
With toast that sings and bacon dances,
Life's too silly for second chances!

The sun yawns big, wearing a grin,
As kittens in pajamas spin.
They tumble and roll through the day,
In a world that's brighter than cliché.

A quirky parade of mismatched socks,
Skips through puddles, around the clocks.
With each splash, we find pure delight,
Living this dream, everything feels right.

So let's toast to life, our quirks and cheer,
For every hiccup, we hold dear.
When the curtains fall, we take a bow,
And laugh in the glow of the here and now!

Chasing Rainbows into Forever

Two squirrels in tutus twirl with glee,
Bounding over rainbows, wild and free.
They chase the colors with gleaming eyes,
Pretending to surf on cotton-candy skies.

Bubblegum storms and licorice trees,
Brought giddy laughter, carried by the breeze.
With jellyfish clouds and marshmallow moon,
Each moment feels like a funny cartoon.

The sun plays tag with a cheeky breeze,
As rowdy raindrops tickle our knees.
Jogging with ducks in a flamboyant race,
Life's a carnival, full of grace.

At the end of the trail, what do we find?
Happiness painted in colors combined.
A confetti blast, a joyful cheer,
Chasing dreams with friends, so near!

A Journey's Reward

A tortoise with wheels zooms down the lane,
Wearing shades and a loud airplane!
Giggling hedgehogs join for the ride,
Through fields of daisies, wide-eyed with pride.

Socks that mismatch and hats askew,
Every stumble just adds to the view.
We collect our giggles like shiny stones,
Each snag a tale, 'til we're oohing moans.

At the finish line, a cake made of cheese,
Served with hot chocolate and warm summer breeze.
We toast to the clumsy and joyful strife,
Celebrating the fun of this whimsical life.

With every laugh, our hearts grow light,
Here's to our journey, a charming sight.
Where friends are the treasure, laughter's our gold,
In a merry adventure, our tales unfold!

Flourishing in Harmony

In a garden where giggles bloom,
Laughter dances, dispelling gloom.
Bees dress in ties, buzzing with glee,
As flowers chat over cups of tea.

Dancing daisies, a polka parade,
Twist and twirl in sunshine's shade.
Worms in tuxedos, digging with might,
Planning a party under the moonlight.

The squirrels debate who jumps the best,
While the trees wear hats, feeling blessed.
A symphony of joy fills the air,
Harmonious laughter, there's joy to spare.

With nature's humor, all find delight,
In a world where everything feels right.
Flourishing smiles, forever stay,
In this quirky land, come laugh and play.

The Light at the End of the Tunnel

In a tunnel so dark, we took a dive,
Tripping over shadows, we barely survived.
Then a glimmer appeared, oh what a sight,
Turns out it's just a raccoon with a light.

He pointed his paw and offered a snack,
A picnic of pickles, what a bold hack!
With laughter we feasted, what a weird spree,
In this strange tunnel, we felt so free.

The echoes of giggles rang off the walls,
As we tumbled and danced, our spirits enthralled.
Emerging from darkness, with crumbs on our face,
The raccoon waved goodbye, oh what a grace.

At the end of our journey, we finally cheered,
For the bright little moments we always revered.
Who knew a raccoon could brighten our plight,
At the end of the tunnel, it finally felt right.

Chapters of Joy

Each page we turn, a chuckle or two,
In stories of mishaps, it's always anew.
The hero trips, spills milk on the floor,
And ducks wear hats, always wanting more.

A dragon named Fred, with a very small roar,
Saves kittens from trees—what a noble score!
But trips on his tail, gives a sigh and a pout,
Our laughter erupts, what's this book about?

The villain, a bunny, steals carrots galore,
Only to find out they're not meant to bore.
He sets off a chase, with the carrots in tow,
The twists and the turns, what a delightful show!

With each chapter flipped, our hearts take a leap,
As giggles and joy take a jolly sweep.
In this whimsical tale, come join our ride,
Through pages of laughter, let joy be your guide.

The Whimsical Farewell

A hat-wearing cat did tip his brim,
As friends gathered close, the lights grew dim.
They conjured up spells with a flick and a twirl,
And all of their wishes began to unfurl.

A sparkly parade of strange critters came,
Dancing in circles, calling out names.
With banjos and trumpets, a raucous sound,
In the fanciest farewell the world had found.

The trees were swaying, feeling the beat,
Crickets provided a rhythm so sweet.
With cake made of clouds and sodas that fizz,
Each laugh and each cheer was a whirlwind whiz.

As the night turned to day, they waved their goodbye,
With wishes for luck that soared high in the sky.
In this odd little tale of joy without end,
A whimsical farewell to remember, my friend.

www.ingramcontent.com/pod-product-compliance
Lightning Source LLC
LaVergne TN
LVHW050400030125
800298LV00004B/640